Make Your Own Science Experiment!

Let's Make a

Fossil

by Katie Chanez

NORWOOD HOUSE PRESS

Norwood House Press

For information regarding Norwood House Press, please visit our website at:
www.norwoodhousepress.com or call 866-565-2900.

PHOTO CREDITS: Cover ©: Red Line Editorial; © Bas van der Pluijm/Shutterstock Images, 14; © Danny Ye/Shutterstock Images, 17; © Inspired By Maps/Shutterstock Images, 7; © jaboo2foto/iStockphoto, 11; © paleontologist natural/Shutterstock Images, 4; © Philippe Gouveia/iStockphoto, 8; © Red Line Editorial, 19, 21, 22, 23, 24, 25, 26, 27, 28; © stihii/Shutterstock Images, 13

Hardcover ISBN: 978-1-68450-841-9
Paperback ISBN: 978-1-68404-621-8

LIBRARY OF CONGRESS CATALOGING-IN-PUBLICATION DATA
Names: Chanez, Katie, author.
Title: Let's make a fossil / by Katie Chanez.
Description: Chicago : Norwood House Press, [2021] | Series: Make your own : science experiment! | Includes index. | Audience: Grades 2-3
Identifiers: LCCN 2019058384 (print) | LCCN 2019058385 (ebook) | ISBN 9781684508419 (hardcover) | ISBN 9781684046218 (paperback) | ISBN 9781684046270 (pdf)
Subjects: LCSH: Fossils--Juvenile literature. | Science projects--Juvenile literature. | Science--Experiments--Juvenile literature.
Classification: LCC QE714.5 .C48 2021 (print) | LCC QE714.5 (ebook) | DDC 560--dc23
LC record available at https://lccn.loc.gov/2019058384
LC ebook record available at https://lccn.loc.gov/2019058385

328N—072020
Manufactured in the United States of America in North Mankato, Minnesota.

Contents

Scientists discover, dig up, and study fossils.

CHAPTER 1

All about Fossils

Fossils are remains of past plant or animal life. The remains have been **preserved**. Scientists study fossils. Fossils teach scientists about **extinct** animals such as dinosaurs. Fossils show how animals have slowly changed over time. They also teach about ancient human life. Without fossils, scientists would know very little about early life on Earth.

Fossils can form in several ways. Sometimes parts of a body are preserved. Some fossils keep **organisms** almost exactly how they were. Scientists can find soft body parts. These parts include skin, hair, and organs. Other fossils are stone versions or **impressions** of organisms. These fossils are often only the hard parts of bodies. Hard parts include bones, teeth, and shells.

Bodies of animals may freeze. Some parts of the world are cold all year. Dead bodies in these places can stay frozen for hundreds or even thousands of years. Other parts of the world are very dry. Bodies in these places can dry out. They become natural **mummies**. Mummies can last for thousands of years. Both freezing and drying

These fish remains were preserved in rock.

can preserve parts of an animal that normally **decay**. Two examples are skin and hair.

Sometimes animals or plants get stuck in sticky substances. Tar is one of these substances. Animals may step into tar. They get stuck

Amber is often a yellow-orange color. It is see-through.

and sink. The tar preserves their bones. Bugs, plants, and even small animals can also get stuck in sap. Sap comes from trees or other plants. The sap hardens into **amber**. It traps the organisms inside. Entire organisms can be found in amber.

Most fossils form when **minerals** replace an organism's cells. An organism dies. It is buried by mud or sand. This mud or sand is called **sediment**. Water enters the organism. The water is full of minerals. The organism's cells fill with the water. The water then turns into a gas. It leaves its minerals behind. This process creates a stone version of the organism. This type of fossil often preserves only hard parts. These fossils are usually very detailed.

Sometimes, water **dissolves** the organism that is buried. This leaves an empty space in the sediment. The space is shaped like the organism. Over time, the sediment hardens into solid rock. This type of fossil is called a mold. Molds can fill with other types of sediment. This forms a second fossil. The second fossil is called a cast.

Sometimes scientists make their own casts in mold fossils. This allows scientists to recreate what the organisms looked like.

Few organisms become fossils when they die. The conditions have to be just right. Many fossils form near rivers. The moving water quickly covers an animal in mud. The faster an animal is buried, the less decay happens. The animal is more likely to become a fossil. Most fossils are of bones or shells. These materials are hard. They do not decay as quickly as soft parts. For example, skin is soft. It decays quickly. Animals with soft bodies rarely become fossils. One example is worms. Their bodies decay rapidly. They have to be buried by mud very quickly to become fossils.

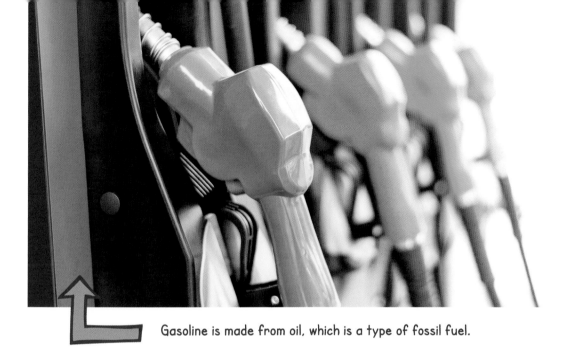

Gasoline is made from oil, which is a type of fossil fuel.

Plants can also become fossils. But they must be buried quickly. Coal is a type of plant fossil. Coal formed in ancient swamps. Plants died and fell into the swamp. More plants grew and died. Layers built up. Over time, the plants turned into coal. People burn coal to make electricity. Coal is a **fossil fuel**.

The most common fossils are of tiny **microorganisms**. These are living things that can only be seen under a microscope. Scientists use these fossils to learn what the ocean was like millions of years ago.

Not all fossils are made from the remains of organisms. Sometimes fossils form from footprints, eggs, nests, or animal droppings. These fossils are called trace fossils. These tell scientists how organisms lived.

People find fossils in many ways. **Paleontologists** are scientists who study fossils. They find and **excavate** fossils. Sometimes rain or rivers uncover fossils. The water washes away the rocks and dirt. Often, people find fossils by accident. People find them while digging for construction projects. They also find them while farming or mining.

A Fossil Forms

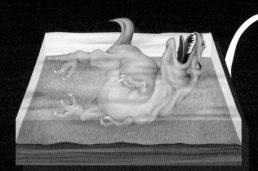 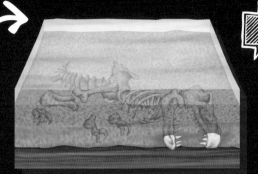 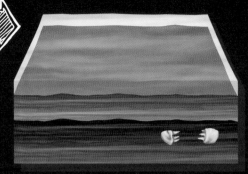

A dinosaur dies in a river. Moving water covers it in mud.

Minerals replace the bones.

The mud hardens into rock.

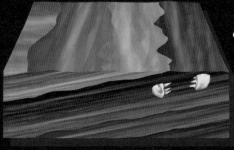

Earth's movements bring the fossil to the surface.

Water uncovers the fossil.

Ancient oceans preserved many organisms in mud.

CHAPTER 2

Make Your Own Fossil

Natural fossils can take between a few hours and a few years to form. Then they can last for thousands of years. You will make your own fossil with common household items.

Mold fossils form when an organism is buried in soft sediment, such as mud. The mud holds the shape of the organism after it dissolves. The mud hardens into rock. You need something that will hold its shape. Modeling clay is a soft material. It will hold the shape of your organism. It will also harden over time. Then you can keep your mold.

Fossils usually form from the remains of living things. Plant leaves are from living things. But they are very thin. It would be hard to make a fossil out of them. Such a thin fossil would break. Small plastic animals, such as toy dinosaurs, look like living things. They are hard. They will make good impressions in the clay.

You also need a material to make your cast. The cast will fill the mold. Plaster of paris is a powder made of minerals. It makes a paste when it is mixed with water. It hardens in a few hours. Then you can

Museums use copies of fossils to protect the original fossils.

remove the plaster from the mold. It will keep its shape. Scientists use plaster to make casts. The casts allow scientists to study fossils without damaging them. Museums sometimes use casts to make copies of fossils to display.

Fossils can be hard to find. They are rarely on the surface of the earth. Paleontologists often remove fossils from the rock surrounding them. They must work very carefully. Sometimes fossils can be damaged or destroyed. The paleontologists use tools such as paintbrushes and small picks. These help scientists carefully clean the rock away from fossils. You can bury your fossils. Then you can excavate them just like a paleontologist!

Materials Checklist

- ✓ Modeling clay
- ✓ Small plastic animals
- ✓ Plaster of paris
- ✓ Water
- ✓ Glass or plastic container
- ✓ Mixing bowl
- ✓ Spoon
- ✓ Sand (optional)
- ✓ Paint brush (optional)
- ✓ Tray or shallow pan (optional)

19

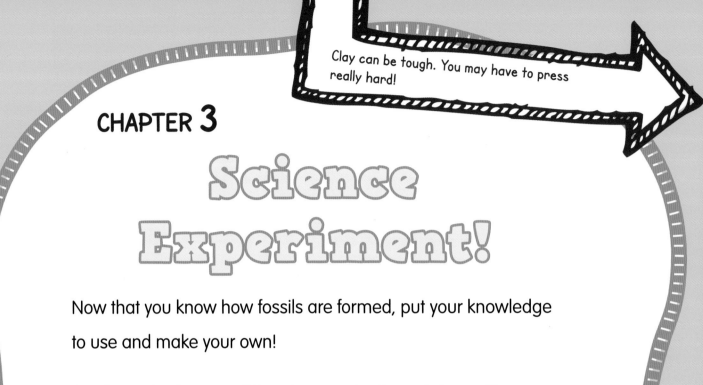

Clay can be tough. You may have to press really hard!

CHAPTER 3

Science Experiment!

Now that you know how fossils are formed, put your knowledge to use and make your own!

1. Cover the bottom of the glass or plastic container with modeling clay. You need a thick layer. It should be thicker than your plastic animals.

2. Press the plastic animals firmly into the clay. Do not cover them with clay.

3. Carefully remove the toys from the clay. A clear shape should be left behind. If not, smooth the clay flat and try again.

4. In a mixing bowl, mix plaster of paris with water. You need enough to fill the shapes. Stir until the plaster is smooth and slightly thick.

5. Spoon the plaster into the shapes left by the toys.

6. Let the plaster dry overnight.

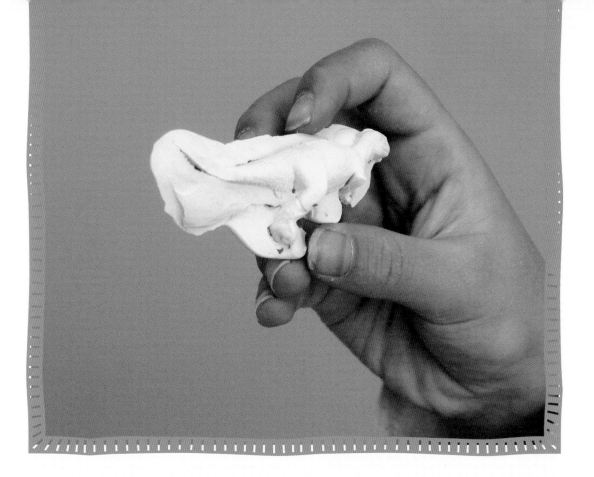

7. Have an adult help you carefully remove the plaster from the clay.

8. If you want, you can pour sand in a tray. Then you can bury your fossils. Use a paint brush to reveal your fossils just like a paleontologist!

Make It Better!

Congratulations! You have made a fossil. Now see if there are ways to improve it. Use any of these changes and see how they improve your fossil.

- You used plaster of paris to make your fossil. What other materials could you make your fossil out of?

- Fossils can be made from bones, eggs, plants, footprints, and more. What other items can you use to shape your fossil?

Can you think of any ways that you could improve or change your fossil to make it better?

Glossary

amber (AM-bur): Hard, fossilized tree sap.

decay (duh-KAY): To break down over time.

dissolves (di-ZOLVZ): Breaks apart and seems to disappear when mixed with a liquid.

excavate (EX-kuh-vayt): To dig something out and remove it.

extinct (ek-STINGKT): Having died out.

fossil fuel (FOSS-uhl FYOO-uhl): A fuel such as coal, oil, or natural gas, formed from prehistoric plant and animal remains.

impressions (im-PRESH-unz): Images or forms pressed on the surface of something.

microorganisms (my-croh-OR-guh-niz-uhmz): Living things that can only be seen with a microscope.

minerals (MIN-ur-uhls): Substances found in nature that are not plant or animal.

mummies (MUH-meez): Bodies that are preserved by being dried out.

organisms (OR-guh-ni-zuhmz): Living things, such as plants and animals.

paleontologists (pay-lee-on-TAH-luh-gists): Scientists who study fossils.

preserved (pri-ZERVD): Kept in its original state.

sediment (SEH-duh-muhnt): Rocks, sand, or mud at the bottom of a body of water.

For More Information

Books

Kate Waters. *Curious about Fossils.* New York, NY: Grosset & Dunlap, 2016. This book explores how fossils form and recounts important fossil discoveries.

Ruth Owen. *Fossils: What Dinosaurs Left Behind.* New York, NY: Bearport Publishing, 2019. Readers learn about the types of fossils left behind by dinosaurs and how the fossils formed.

Scott D. Sampson. *You Can Be a Paleontologist!* Washington, DC: National Geographic, 2017. This book explores the work paleontologists do as they find fossils.

Websites

DK Find Out! Fossils (https://www.dkfindout.com/us/dinosaurs-and-prehistoric-life/fossils/) This website discusses different types of fossils, how they form, and where they can be found.

National Geographic Kids: Dino Death Pit (https://kids.nationalgeographic.com/explore/science/dino-death-pit/) This article discusses a fossil pit found in the Gobi Desert in China and how its dinosaur fossils came to be there.

Wonderopolis: What Is a Paleontologist? (https://www.wonderopolis.org/wonder/what-is-a-paleontologist) This website explains what paleontologists are and the kinds of research they do.

Index

About the Author

Katie Chanez is a children's book writer and editor originally from Iowa. She enjoys writing fiction, playing with her cat, and petting friendly dogs. Katie now lives and works in Minnesota.